A Look at Space

# The Sun

by Rebecca Sabelko

BLASTOFF! BEGINNERS,
AN IMPRINT OF
BELLWETHER MEDIA
BY FLUTTERBEE

**Blastoff! Beginners** are developed by literacy experts and educators to meet the needs of early readers. These engaging informational texts support young children as they begin reading about their world. Through simple language and high frequency words paired with crisp, colorful photos, Blastoff! Beginners launch young readers into the universe of independent reading.

## Sight Words in This Book

| | | | | |
|---|---|---|---|---|
| a | do | it | on | they |
| and | has | made | our | too |
| are | in | make | out | |
| day | is | of | the | |

This edition first published in 2027 by Bellwether Media, Inc.



For information regarding permission, write to Bellwether Media, Inc., Attention: Permissions Department, 3500 American Blvd W, Suite 150, Bloomington, MN 55431.

Library of Congress Cataloging-in-Publication Data is available at www.loc.gov or upon request from the publisher.

ISBN: 9798893049947 (hardcover)
ISBN: 9798898802790 (paperback)
ISBN: 9798898801366 (ebook)

Editor: Suzane Nguyen    Designer: Laura Sowers

Printed in the United States of America, North Mankato, MN.

# Table of Contents

# The Summer Sun

It is a hot summer day. The sun shines bright.

# A Star

The sun
is a star.
It is made
of **gas**.

It is round
and bright!

It is the only
star in our
**solar system.**

sun
Mars
Earth
Venus
Mercury
Jupiter
solar system

Planets move around the sun. Moons do too!

moon

sun

planet

# The Hot Sun

The sun makes **energy**. It is very hot!

The sun
has sunspots.
They are dark,
cool places.

sunspots

**Flares** shoot out light and energy.

flare

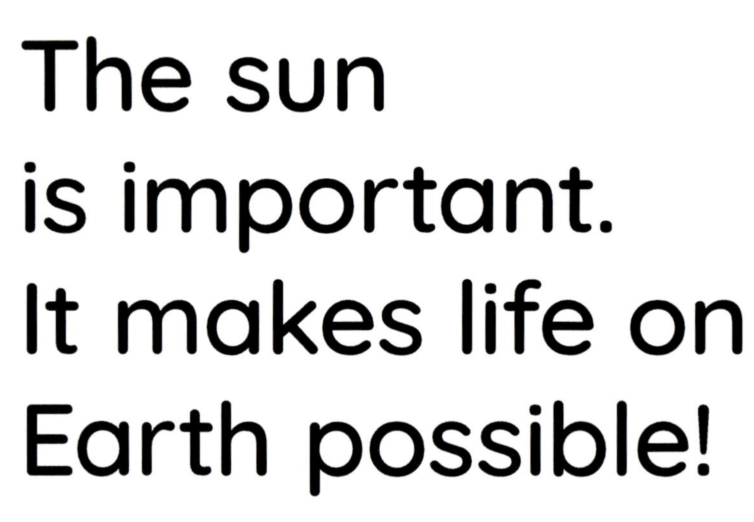

The sun
is important.
It makes life on
Earth possible!

# About the Sun

## The Sun in the Solar System

## Parts of the Sun

energy sunspots flares

# Glossary

**energy**

light and heat made by the sun

**flares**

bursts of light and energy

**gas**

something that does not keep its size or shape

**solar system**

the sun and everything that moves around it

# To Learn More

## ON THE WEB

## FACTSURFER

Factsurfer.com gives you a safe, fun way to find more information.

1. Go to www.factsurfer.com.
2. Enter "the sun" into the search box and click 🔍.
3. Select your book cover to see a list of related content.

# Index



The images in this book are reproduced through the courtesy of: wasan, front cover, p. 22 (sun, Uranus); gizemg, pp. 3, 22 (Venus); alinamd, pp. 4-5; NASA/J PL-Caltech/ GSFC, pp. 6-7; lukszczepanski, pp. 8-9; Lithiumphoto, p. 10; sanirimpan, pp. 10-11; sdecoret, pp. 12-13; Artsiom P, pp. 14-15, 22 (energy), 23 (gas); NASA Goddard, pp. 16-17, 18-19; Ирина Гутыряк, p. 20; CreativeSuburb, pp. 20-21; SN, p. 22 (Mercury); NASA Goddard Space Flight Center Image by Reto Stöckl/ Wikipedia, p. 22 (Earth); Kevin Gill/ Wikipedia, p. 22 (Mars); MARUF Ahmed, p. 22 (Jupiter); Trym, p. 22 (Saturn); Thomas, p. 22 (Neptune); NASA, p. 22 (sunspots); mgs, p. 22 (flares); Tryfonov, p. 23 (energy); NASA/ Wikipedia, p. 23 (flares); arinahabich, p. 23 (solar system).